THE
WANDERER'S
JOURNAL

THE WANDERER'S JOURNAL

GUIDED PROMPTS FOR
Hikers, Backpackers, and Explorers

JENNIFER DOEHRING

Countryman Press

An Imprint of W. W. Norton & Company
Independent Publishers Since 1923

THE WANDERER'S JOURNAL is a journal template for hikers to use to record their thoughts and experiences on and off the trail. While this book includes a few fun facts and informational illustrations, it is not an instructional text, a technical hiking manual, nor a comprehensive hiking guide. Before embarking on a hike of any duration, the reader is advised to consult sources specifically written to educate hikers about hiking conditions and hazards, appropriate hiking and camping clothing and gear, choosing hiking routes, hiking permits and trail etiquette, setting up camp, and how to handle difficult circumstances on the trail or while camping.

For information about permission to reproduce selections from this book, write to Permissions, Countryman Press, 500 Fifth Avenue, New York, NY 10110

For information about special discounts for bulk purchases, please contact W. W. Norton Special Sales at specialsales@wwnorton.com or 800-233-4830

Manufacturing through Imago
Book design by Allison Chi
Production manager: Devon Zahn

Countryman Press
www.countrymanpress.com

An imprint of W. W. Norton & Company, Inc.
500 Fifth Avenue, New York, NY 10110
www.wwnorton.com

978-1-68268-904-2

10 9 8 7 6 5 4 3 2 1

To Jeff, my favorite hiking partner.

How to Use This Book

This journal is intended to help you to remember small yet magical details, to record opportunities of growth and reflection, and to appreciate and keep track of every hike—short or long. Some prompts are silly, some are practical, and some are more contemplative.

This book has no set order, so please jump around! Pick the prompt that speaks to you at that moment. Some pages are post-hike prompts, and some are prompts you can answer during a break on the trail or in your tent at night. You decide which prompts and pages to fill out and when.

You'll notice that some prompt pages are meant to be an answer-once prompt (though it's your journal—use it anyway you want!), while others are good for a number of different hikes. Pick and choose your way through the book, stopping to answer whatever compels you in the moment.

Unexpected Moments:

Date: 4/22/23

Today on the trail I saw a moose! It was the first time I'd ever seen one. They're so much BIGGER in person than I thought. It was incredible! I got some awesome pictures before it ran off.

Date: 6/2/23

This time of year in Glacier isn't usually so hot. Definitely unexpected for my hike today.

To keep track of each hike's entries, there's an index page at the back where in addition to recording where you hiked, what trail(s) you were on, the weather, who you were with, and other details, you can also indicate which pages in the journal you filled out.

HIKE INDEX

Date _4/22/23_   Place _Denali NP_   Hiked With _Best friend_

Distance _12 miles_   Duration _2 days_   Conditions _Clear and cold_

Backpack ☐   Day Pack ☒   No Pack ☐

Prompt Pages Used _4, 18, 56, 89, 101_

Extra Notes _Alaska is an incredible place, and so much of it is still left to be explored! I need to come back in the summer for more open trails._

Later, when the book is full, it serves as a memory keeper of hikes, triumphs, thoughts, companions, and things you saw, felt, and did along the way.

So what are you waiting for? Get out there and explore!

"In every walk with nature, one receives far more than he seeks."
—JOHN MUIR

What's in your backpack for this hike?

Essentials:

Oddities:

Comfort:

Wish I had:

Over time, small details can be forgotten. **Use these spaces to capture your favorite moments on your hikes.**

Date:

Date:

Date:

Date:

Date:

Date:

The farther away things are, the lighter (or more blue) they can seem. This is because light particles scatter in what is called the Rayleigh Effect. **What did you see farthest away today?**

Closest?

What did you think about most during your hike?

Who did you think about most during your hike?

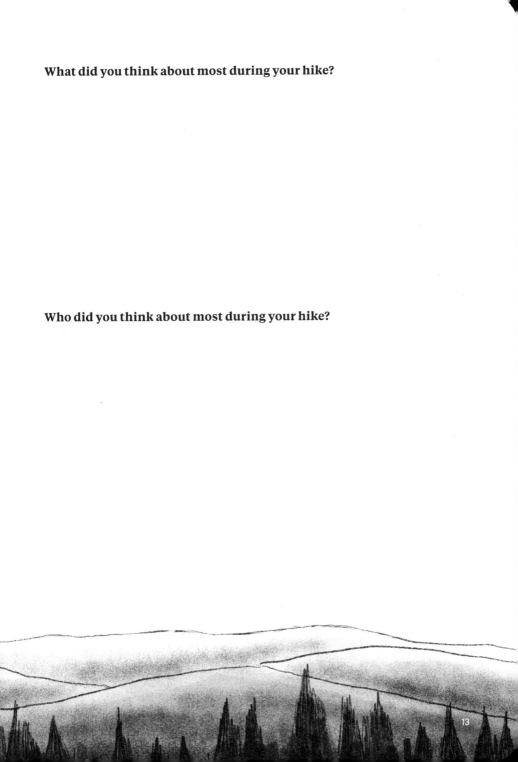

An Elevation Map of Your Day

Example

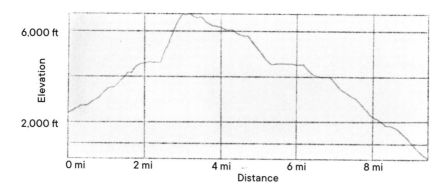

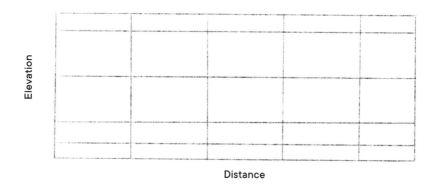

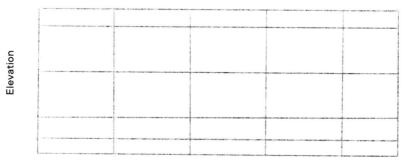

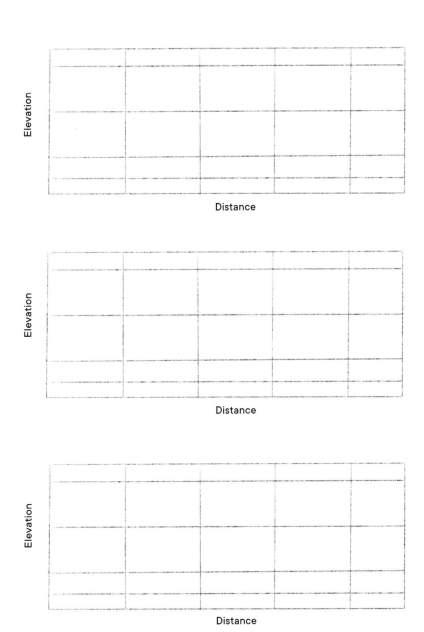

Would you rather:

Hike up or down a mountain?

Camp next to people or with no other people around?

Hike a long and moderate trail or a short and intense one?

Hike in the desert or in the forest?

Hike in the rain or in the snow?

Hiking is the answer.
Who cares what the question is.

With nature comes insects. **What were you bitten or stung by on this hike?**

Date:

Date:

Date:

Date:

Common Wisdom for Most Insect Bites and Stings

- Remove the stinger or hairs if still in the skin.
- Take an over-the-counter antihistamine to help with allergic reactions.
- Carry pain-relieving creams in case of a bite or sting.
- Watch for severe symptoms: impaired speech, muscle spasms, vomiting, etc.

Date:

Date:

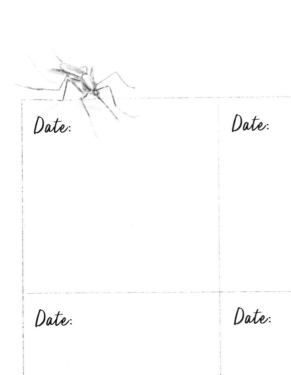

Date:

Date:

- Wash the infected area with soap and water, if possible, and then apply an antibiotic ointment.
- Use a cold compress to reduce swelling and pain.
- Try not to scratch or itch the area, as it can become infected.
- If the bite or sting is on an arm or leg, keep the area elevated to help reduce swelling.

What things would you bring hiking/backpacking/camping if you didn't have to carry them yourself?

Epic Hike

Today, I went on a hiking adventure in _____.

Armed with my trusty_____, I set off on the trail, eager to explore

_____.

As I walked, I couldn't help but notice _____,

_____, and _____.

I continued to venture deeper on the trail, and I was greeted by _____

_____.

It made me _____ because I had only _____ once before.

With each step, the scenery became more _____, and suddenly

I realized that _____.

At one point, I stumbled upon _____ and that

made me _____.

When I finally made it back home, I _____ and

_____.

Today was one of the best hikes I've done because _____

_____.

_____.

_____.

Hiking Rules and Etiquette

- Don't hike off-trail. Often, parks are trying to regrow ecosystems in heavily trampled areas.

- People coming uphill have the right of way.

- Pack it in and pack it out.

- Set up your tent at least 100 feet away from any water source.

- Don't light a fire unless you're sure it's safe and allowed in your area.

- Put any food more than 100 feet away from your tent so animals aren't attracted to your space while you sleep. Use either a bear-proof container or a bear bag that is at least 14 feet off the ground.

Always:

- Be aware of your surroundings.

- Bring extra food; be prepared for anything.

- Check the trail conditions beforehand.

- Carry a first-aid kit.

- Make sure to get the proper permits before you start your hike.

My Personal Hiking Etiquette

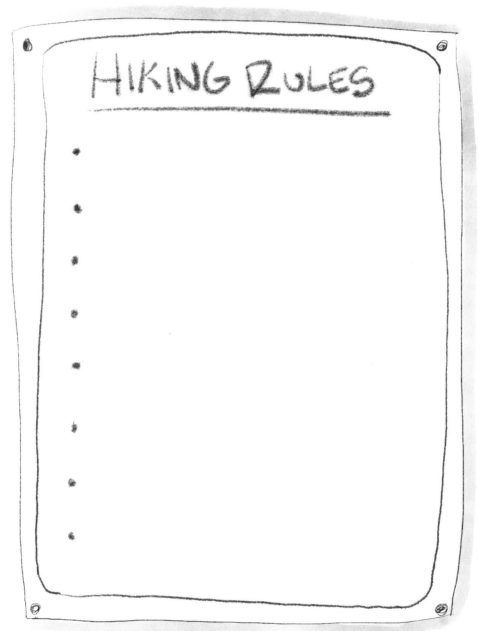

HIKING RULES

-
-
-
-
-
-
-
-

Pet peeves on my hike today. Vent it out!

Unexpected Moments

Date:

Date:

Date:

Date:

Date:

Date:

Roughly 1% of your body's cells are replaced every day (that means over 300 billion cells per day!). Your skin cells turn over every two to four weeks. **With so many fresh starts going on internally, what external do-overs might you want to try before your next hike?**

Describe the color and texture of the dirt you saw today.

Date:

Date:

Date:

Date:

Date:

On this break, stop and engage your five senses. **Write down what you:**

See:

Hear:

Smell:

Touch:

Taste:

Tree Log

Date:

Date:

Date:

Date:

Date:

Date:

Date:

Date:

Pine: long needles
in clusters

Hemlock: short,
flat, soft needles

Spruce: spiky needles
spreading in all directions

When you go out into the woods and you look at the trees,
you see all these different trees. And some of them are bent and some of
them are straight and some of them are evergreens and some of them are
whatever. And you look at the tree and you allow it. You see why it is the way
it is. You sort of understand that it didn't get enough light, and so it turned
that way. And you don't get all emotional about it. You just allow it. You
appreciate the tree. The minute you get near humans, you lose all that.
And you are constantly saying, "you're too this or I'm too this."
That judging mind comes in. And so I practice turning people into
trees. Which means appreciating them just the way they are."

—RAM DASS

Give yourself the kindness you'd give a tree. **Meditate on what has made you *you*, and the ways in which you appreciate who you've become.**

Every hike makes us stronger. **Celebrate this and, after your hike, make a note of where and how you're getting stronger inside and out.**

Miles logged so far this year:

Goals for this year/next year:

Longest trail ever hiked:

Long-distance dream hike:

"The world reveals itself to those who travel on foot."
—WERNER HERZOG

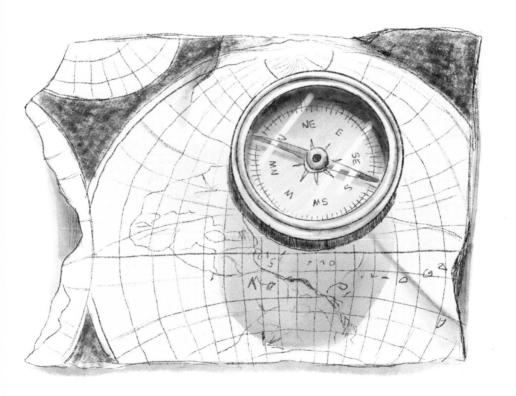

We feel every good hike in our body. **Take a moment to circle or capture where you hurt or ache the most after a hike.** Pay attention to patterns over time—there may be solutions, fixes, or adjustments to be made!

Date:

Date:

Date:

Date:

Date: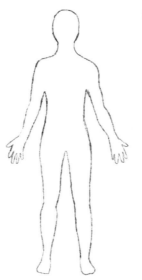

Date: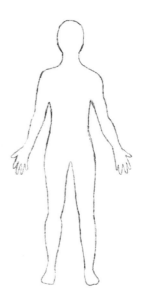

Date: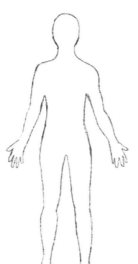

Date: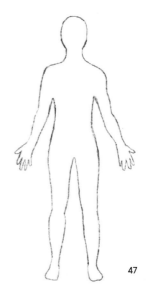

Did you get lost today? How did you get back on track?

Date:

Date:

Date:

Date:

Date:

Date:

Three Ways to Find True North

Look for Polaris, the North Star, in the night sky.
Polaris is directly above the North Pole.

In the desert, the giant barrel cactus
always leans toward the south.

Ants! If you spot an ant hill at the base of
a tree, it's likely to be on the south side.

What are some ways of finding your inner true north?

When you're hiking or camping with a buddy or group . . . **Who took the lead and why?**

What conversations did you have with your hiking buddy, if any?

What was your most difficult moment together?
How did you get past it?

What was your funniest or most memorable moment together?

Hiking/walking spurs creativity. **Use your time to think of inventions that would help you on your next hike. Go wild!**

Need:

Idea for solution:

Need:

Idea for solution:

Need:

Idea for solution:

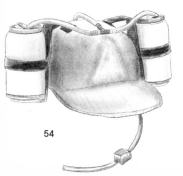

My ideal pack would have:

Outside:

Inside:

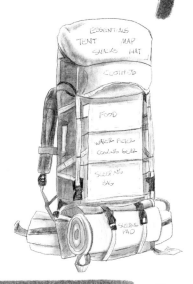

Color challenge. During your hike, try to notice and write down everything you see that is:

Red:

Blue:

Yellow:

Green:

Orange:

Purple:

How has your mood shifted since you got outdoors? Keep track of how long it takes to shift, and what your positive triggers are.

Hike #1:

Hike #2:

Hike #3:

Hike #4:

Hike #5:

Hike #6:

Did you encounter any negative self-talk on your journey? In what ways did you or can you turn those thoughts into constructive ones?

Some moments I felt most alive in my skin during this hike:

Date:

Date:

Date:

Date:

Date:

Date:

Date:

Date:

Photos don't capture exactly how we feel. **Instead of taking a photo today, describe what you wanted to photograph—the details and the feelings. Or, if so inclined, you can sketch it.**

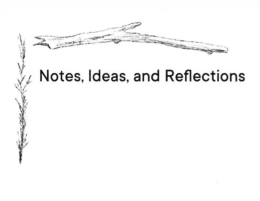

Notes, Ideas, and Reflections

Ebony is the world's darkest wood.
The whitest is holly.

Some fun for overnighters! **What is your most memorable tent-building experience? Worst? (Solo or with a partner)**

What are your tried-and-true methods for building a fire, or what have you seen someone else do that you want to try?

Best campfire meals you've had?

What are your favorite things to do once you're done building your site for the night?

Star spotting . . .

Draw the stars you see at night.

As a bonus, make your own constellation and story.

What were all the sounds you heard last night?

Best campfire recipes or snacks on the move?

Nature can be pretty strange. For example, did you know flowers can hear buzzing bees? **What's the weirdest thing you've opened your hiking tent to see?**

True story.

What post-hike foods are you dreaming about?

Same place, different person . . . **When did you last hike this trail? What's changed in memory or reality? How are you a different person since you were last here?**

Nature is humbling in all the right ways. **At least once during your hike, take a break and use the moment to reflect on what you're grateful for on or off the trail.**

Camping Hacks and Tips to Try on Your Next Adventure

- Dip cotton swabs in wax or Vaseline and store in a zip-top bag for easy fire-starters.

- Dehydrate your favorite coffee concentrate ahead of time and when ready, simply mix with boiling water for a delicious morning coffee.

- Bring extra dry bags—even fog and misty mornings can dampen things.

- Bring sandals so you can switch into them after a long day of hiking to give your feet and blisters a break!

- Pack wet wipes and hand sanitizer for fast and easy cleaning.

My own tips and hacks:

Trees only get 10% of their nutrition from the soil, while 90% is from the atmosphere. In some ways, humans are just like trees. **What things in your personal atmosphere fuel you in your daily life?**

Every hiker feels the miles in their feet. **When you're done for the day, note where your blisters, aches, and raw spots are.** They are badges of a good hike; but if they are in the same spots consistently, you have a footwear issue.

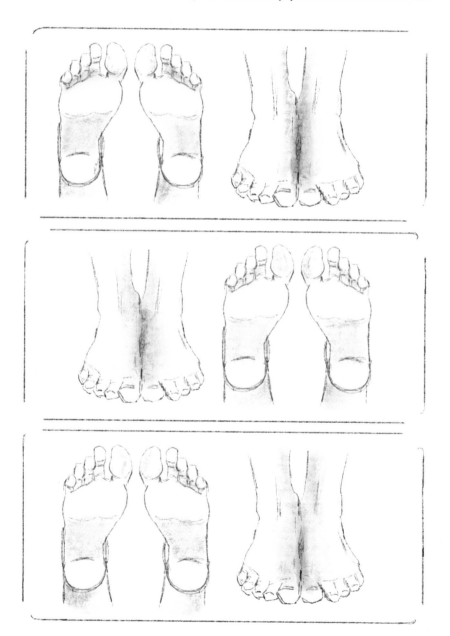

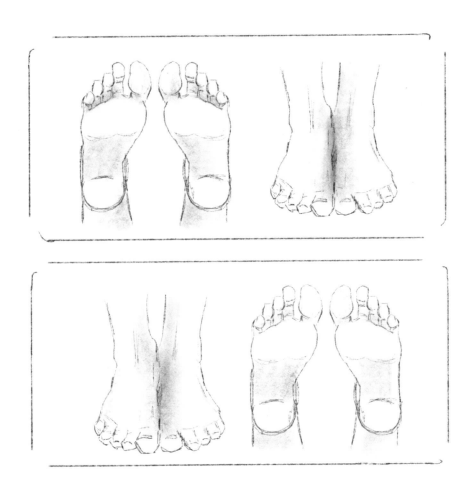

Common Wisdom for Most Blisters and Raw Spots

First, clean the blister as best you can. Then, use an antibiotic ointment to make sure the area doesn't become infected, and cover with a bandage. If you are continuing to hike, for added protection and to prevent further irritation, use moleskin or add an extra layer of gauze and tape to the top.

"Leave the roads; take the trails."

—PYTHAGORAS

Notes, Ideas, and Reflections

List the scariest moment on your hike today.

Date:

Date:

Date:

List the most exhilarating moment on your hike today.

Date:

Date:

Date:

Dirt, mud, snow—the ground has a lot to tell us about animals in the area. **What tracks did you see today?**

Date:	Date:
Date:	Date:

Date:

Date:

Date:

Date:

American crow   Grizzly bear   Whitetail deer

Only 1% of earth's water is safe for human consumption. **What water sources did you see on your hike today?**

Date:

Date:

Date:

Date:

Date:

Always carry a water filter/purifier on your hikes to ensure safe drinking water in case you run out or get lost.

Stop to fix small problems so they don't become bigger in the future.

Reminders!

What to do before my next hike:

Things I saw others using or doing on the hike that I'm curious about:

Food / meals:

Equipment:

Hiking techniques:

Mountains make up one-fifth of the world's landscape. **Use the space to jot down your bucket-list mountains, real or metaphorical. If you have any mountain triumphs, write about them too.**

Bucket list hiking trips! **Circle them or fill them out on the map below!**

Which national parks have you been to?

Circle the ones you've visited!

BRYCE CANYON CANYONLANDS CARLSBAD CAVERNS CAPITOL REEF CHANNEL ISLANDS

CUYAHOGA VALLEY DEATH VALLEY DENALI DRY TORTUGAS EVERGLADES

GLACIER BAY GLACIER GRAND CANYON GRAND TETON GREAT SAND DUNES

GUADALUPE HALEAKALA VOLCANOES HOT SPRINGS INDIANA DUNES

KATMAI KINGS CANYON KENAI FJORDS KOBUK VALLEY LAKE CLARK

BISCAYNE BLACK CANYON CONGAREE CRATER LAKE GATES OF THE ARCTIC

MT RAINIER

 GREAT BASIN

 YELLOWSTONE

 REDWOOD

 ROCKY MOUNTAIN

 ISLE ROYALE

 JOSHUA TREE

 MESA VERDE

 VOYAGERS

 WIND CAVE

 LASSEN VOLCANIC

 MAMMOTH CAVE

 GATEWAY ARCH

 NEW RIVER GORGE

 NORTH CASCADES

 OLYMPIC

 PETRIFIED FOREST

 PINNACLES

 SAGUARO

 SEQUOIA

 SHENANDOAH

 ROOSEVELT

 VIRGIN ISLANDS

 WHITE SANDS

 WRANGELL-ST. ELIAS

 GREAT SMOKEY MOUNTAINS

 YOSEMITE

 ZION

 ACADIA

 AMERICAN SAMOA

 ARCHES

 BADLANDS

BIG BEND

Fungi! They're natural cleaners of the environment. They feed on dead and decaying substances, break down chemical pollutants like oil, and can even filter water! **Did you spot any fungi on your hike today? Make note of where it was growing, then describe it.**

Date:

Date:

Date:

Date:

Date:

Date:

Date:

Studies show that hiking makes us happier in general and less susceptible to depression. Think of your happiest moments on the trail. **What made you smile?**

Date:

Date:

Date:

Date:

Date:

Date:

Date:

"Hike your own hike."
—BEN CRAWFORD

Notes, Ideas, and Reflections

Benefits of hiking: anxiety decreases, muscle fitness improves, brain power boosts!

Camping Trip

My favorite camping trip was with _____

during _____.

The campsite was in _____ and the air

was filled with _____. I even heard _____

_____!

I unpacked _____, _____,

and plenty of _____.

As the sun began to set, I gathered my _____

and started to _____.

I made a campfire out of _____ and _____.

After a satisfying meal of_____ and _____,

I made a bed with my _____and fell asleep to the sound of

_____.

I woke up in the morning with_____, and stepped out

of my tent to hear _____, which _____.

I couldn't resist _____ before it was time to pack up

and head _____.

I will always remember this trip, because_____

_____.

If you could name the trail you are/were hiking today, what would it be?

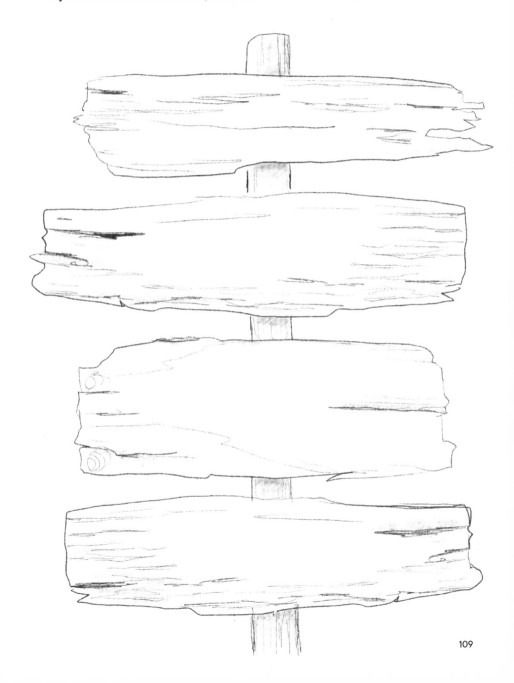

Always dress for the conditions! **For a warm-weather hike, the best outfit for me is:**

Head gear:

Outfit:

Footwear:

For colder hiking conditions, the best outfit for me is:

Head gear:

Outfit:

Footwear:

Many hikers underestimate the power of nature and weather. **Describe a time when you were on a hike and something unpredictable happened for the worse.**

And for the better?

Walking helps with problem-solving. Before you set out today, choose something you want to work through and direct your thoughts to it over the course of your hike. **Capture your *Eureka!* moments here, or things you want to explore post-hike.**

Date:

Date:

Date:

Date:

Date:

Date:

Would you rather:
Hike the Pacific Crest Trail or the Appalachian Trail?

Hike in scorching sun or freezing winds?

Pack light and wear the same clothes every day or carry extra clothes for a week?

Come face to face with a bear or a mountain lion?

Take a camping trip to see the New England autumn leaves or California's spring wildflower superbloom?

The start of a river is called the source; the end of a river is called the mouth.
Did you have any river or water crossings today? How did you get through them?

Date:

Date:

Date:

Date:

Date:

What have been your favorite features on your hikes? Were they waterfalls? Or a view? Do your favorites change depending on the terrain?

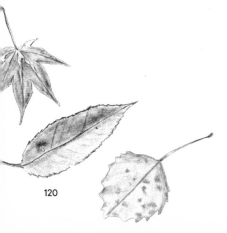

How far into a hike are you before you feel like your full self again?

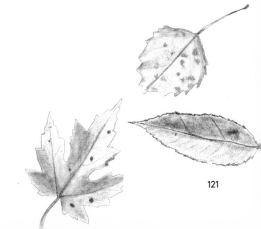

HIKE INDEX

Date_____ Place_____ Hiked With_____

Distance_____ Duration_____ Conditions_____

Backpack ❏ Day Pack ❏ No Pack ❏

Prompt Pages Used_____

Extra Notes_____

_____

_____

HIKE INDEX

Date_____ Place_____ Hiked With_____

Distance_____ Duration_____ Conditions_____

Backpack ❏ Day Pack ❏ No Pack ❏

Prompt Pages Used_____

Extra Notes_____

_____

_____

HIKE INDEX

Date_____ Place_____ Hiked With_____

Distance_____ Duration_____ Conditions_____

Backpack ❏ Day Pack ❏ No Pack ❏

Prompt Pages Used_____

Extra Notes_____

_____

_____

HIKE INDEX

Date_____ Place_____ Hiked With_____

Distance_____ Duration_____ Conditions_____

Backpack ❏ Day Pack ❏ No Pack ❏

Prompt Pages Used_____

Extra Notes_____

_____

_____

HIKE INDEX

Date_____ Place_____ Hiked With_____

Distance_____ Duration_____ Conditions_____

Backpack ❏ Day Pack ❏ No Pack ❏

Prompt Pages Used_____

Extra Notes_____

_____

_____

HIKE INDEX

Date_____ Place_____ Hiked With_____

Distance_____ Duration_____ Conditions_____

Backpack ❏ Day Pack ❏ No Pack ❏

Prompt Pages Used_____

Extra Notes_____

_____

_____

HIKE INDEX

Date_____ Place_____ Hiked With_____

Distance_____ Duration_____ Conditions_____

Backpack ❑ Day Pack ❑ No Pack ❑

Prompt Pages Used_____

Extra Notes_____

_____

_____

HIKE INDEX

Date_____ Place_____ Hiked With_____

Distance_____ Duration_____ Conditions_____

Backpack ❑ Day Pack ❑ No Pack ❑

Prompt Pages Used_____

Extra Notes_____

_____

_____

HIKE INDEX

Date_____ Place_____ Hiked With_____

Distance_____ Duration_____ Conditions_____

Backpack ❑ Day Pack ❑ No Pack ❑

Prompt Pages Used_____

Extra Notes_____

_____

_____

HIKE INDEX

Date_____ Place_____ Hiked With_____

Distance_____ Duration_____ Conditions_____

Backpack ❏   Day Pack ❏   No Pack ❏

Prompt Pages Used_____

Extra Notes_____

_____

_____

HIKE INDEX

Date_____ Place_____ Hiked With_____

Distance_____ Duration_____ Conditions_____

Backpack ❏   Day Pack ❏   No Pack ❏

Prompt Pages Used_____

Extra Notes_____

_____

_____

HIKE INDEX

Date_____ Place_____ Hiked With_____

Distance_____ Duration_____ Conditions_____

Backpack ❏   Day Pack ❏   No Pack ❏

Prompt Pages Used_____

Extra Notes_____

_____

_____

HIKE INDEX

Date_____ Place_____ Hiked With_____

Distance_____ Duration_____ Conditions_____

Backpack ❏ Day Pack ❏ No Pack ❏

Prompt Pages Used_____

Extra Notes_____

_____

_____

HIKE INDEX

Date_____ Place_____ Hiked With_____

Distance_____ Duration_____ Conditions_____

Backpack ❏ Day Pack ❏ No Pack ❏

Prompt Pages Used_____

Extra Notes_____

_____

_____

HIKE INDEX

Date_____ Place_____ Hiked With_____

Distance_____ Duration_____ Conditions_____

Backpack ❏ Day Pack ❏ No Pack ❏

Prompt Pages Used_____

Extra Notes_____

_____

_____

HIKE INDEX

Date_____ Place_____ Hiked With_____

Distance_____ Duration_____ Conditions_____

Backpack ❏ Day Pack ❏ No Pack ❏

Prompt Pages Used_____

Extra Notes_____

_____

_____

HIKE INDEX

Date_____ Place_____ Hiked With_____

Distance_____ Duration_____ Conditions_____

Backpack ❏ Day Pack ❏ No Pack ❏

Prompt Pages Used_____

Extra Notes_____

_____

_____

HIKE INDEX

Date_____ Place_____ Hiked With_____

Distance_____ Duration_____ Conditions_____

Backpack ❏ Day Pack ❏ No Pack ❏

Prompt Pages Used_____

Extra Notes_____

_____

_____

Author's Note

Hiking/backpacking is by far the most powerful and positive activity in my life. It's wholesome, peaceful, and restorative. Anytime I need to quiet my mind, settle my soul, or enable my creativity, nature is the cure. When I watch the plants move, when I listen to the wind, when I stop and just be, I soak in every raw element. Problems that I have back in the busy human world melt away and seem trivial.

When I am reminded of how all-consuming nature is, and how insignificant I am in the grand scheme of things, that's pure bliss for me. I'm happily humbled. Whether I'm doing a day walk near my house, or a 5-night, 60-mile backpacking trek, the outcome is the same. I may be dusty and dirty on the outside, but on the inside, I am cleansed, tranquil, rejuvenated, and ready to take on the world.

I hope you enjoyed using this book and took the time to really see, to be present in your surroundings, and to capture special moments and thoughts in these pages. I hope you found your own humbled bliss. This book will help you remember the small yet magical details of every outing and to appreciate every hike, short or long, for years to come.

See you out on the trail next time.

—Jennifer Doehring

About the Author

JENNIFER DOEHRING is an artist and illustrator living in Southern California. When she's not creating art or writing funny stories for kids, she's out in nature, traveling the world, and backpacking in as many national parks as possible.